D0389153

For my wife, Monika
—K.A.

Text copyright © 1997 by Random House, Inc.
Photographs copyright © 1997 by NBM Bahner Studios, A.G.
All rights reserved under International and Pan-American Copyright
Conventions. Published in the United States by Random House, Inc.,
New York, and simultaneously in Canada by Random House of Canada
Limited, Toronto.

http://www.randomhouse.com/

ISBN: 0-679-88408-4

Library of Congress Catalog Card Number: 97-65947

LIFE FAVORS is a trademark of Random House, Inc.

Printed in the United States of America 10 9 8 7 6 5 4 3 2 1

These Things I Love

PHOTOGRAPHS BY

Kim Anderson

WRITTEN BY *Heather Lowenberg*

LIFE FAVORS™

Random House 🏠 New York

*T*hese are the
things I love...

An ice cream cone on
a warm spring day.
The secret you whisper
before riding away.

*S*winging lazily
all afternoon.
Singing along
to a silly old tune.

*T*ogether watching
the ships set sail.
Getting a letter
in the mail.

Quiet time with
my favorite book.
Falling asleep in
a warm, cozy nook.

*F*eeding the birds and watching them fly.

Shopping for hours—there's so much to buy!

A sweet-smelling rose,
a funny clown nose...

On a hot summer day, cooling off with the hose!

Taking a trip to a
faraway land.
Walking together and
holding your hand.

*S*plashing around
in a sun-dappled lake.
A birthday party
with ice cream and cake.

A baby chick,
soft to the touch.
A kiss on the cheek
means oh so much!

A favorite toy
I held so tight.
While dreaming
sweet dreams all
through the night.

Of all the things
I love, it's true.
The dearest of
them all is YOU!